2-D LINE

GRAPHS

ON

MATLAB

Daniel Okoh and Eric Nwokolo

Preface

Doing graphics with MATLAB can be interesting, the results look quite appealing, and a generality of users prefer it for it's robustness and portability: Graphics in MATLAB can be tweaked to take different desired looks, and can be easily exported into various other applications. This book is a very modest 1-Chapter guide on how to use MATLAB to develop 2-D static graphics. Lots of examples and illustrations have been used to enhance readers' understanding of the subject.

For the sake of clarity, we will explain here that 2-D graphics are those that are usually illustrated on just two axes (say, x-axis and y-axis). In contrast, the 3-D graphics use an additional axis. It is also important for readers to understand that 2-D graphics could be more appropriate for some kind of study, and 3-D for others. This book will concentrate on 2-D line graphs, while the next book in this series will be for 3-D graphs.

Table of Contents

Chapter 1

2-D Line Plots

1.1 The plot Function

2-D line plots are created in MATLAB using the 'plot' function. Very precisely, suppose we want to plot a graph of x against y, then we simply say: plot(x,y)

For sure, x and y has to be predefined; there has to be some data or values they represent. These data could be already existing data, or data to be generated on MATLAB. If the data already exists, users can simply copy/import them into MATLAB. Our previous books titled MATLAB SCRIPTING & FILE PROCESSING and INTRODUCTION TO MATLAB FOR BEGINNERS will be helpful on how to do these.

If however the data is to be generated on MATLAB, then this can be done in a way similar to the illustration below.

Let's have a script which plots x against y for the following definitions for x and y:

x is a row of numbers from 0 to 360 in steps of 10, and y is a row of numbers corresponding to the sines (in degrees) of the numbers in x. The script is as below:

```
x=0:10:360
y=sind(x)
plot(x,y)
```

And the result is as illustrated below.

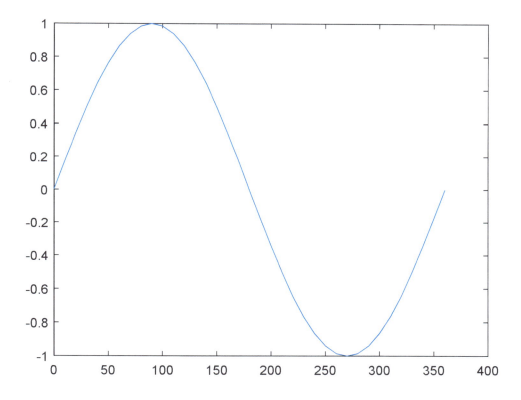

We can now start tweaking the graph to take different looks. For instance, the graph above only shows the line connecting the plotted points, but does not show the points. We can show the points in asterisk (*) if we replace the 3rd line of the script with this:

plot(x,y,'*')

And we get the following plot:

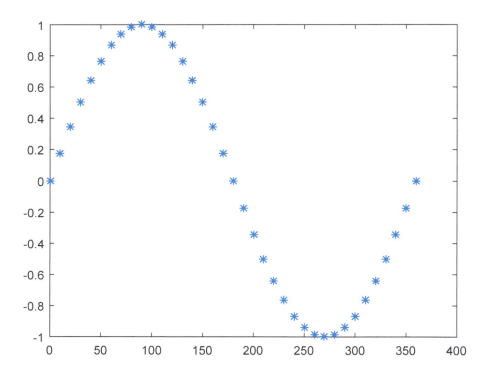

The following are other marker types we can use instead of the asterisk.

Marker Type	How to specify in MATLAB
Circle	o
Cross	x
Square	s
Plus sign	+
Diamond	d
Dot (or point)	.
Pentagram (5-pointed star)	p
Hexagram (6-pointed star)	h
Upward-pointing triangle	^
Downward-pointing triangle	v
Right-pointing triangle	>
Left-pointing triangle	<

For instance, if we need circles instead of asterisks, we use:

plot(x,y, 'o')

And we get:

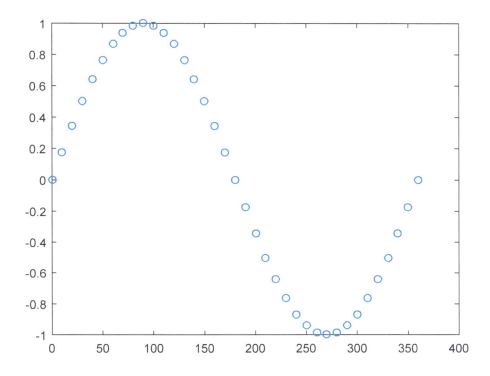

Something else we may want to do is to connect the points with a line, to do this, we use the following (notice it is the included – sign that does this):

plot(x,y,'-*')

The result is as below:

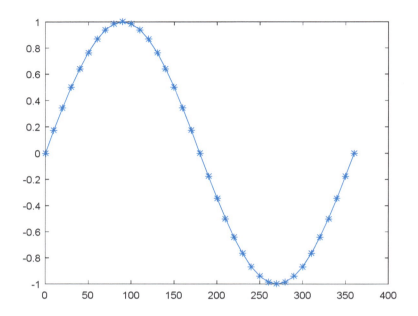

Now you could guess rightly what the following will do:

plot(x,y, '-o')

If you pictured the plot below, then you are right!

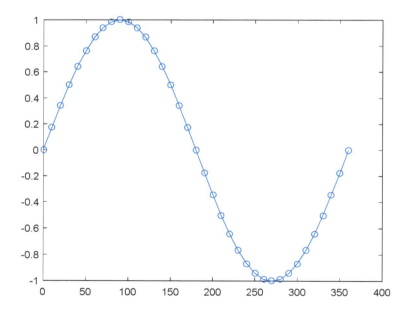

Interestingly, we can also change the width or thickness of the line by extending the code as follows:

plot(x,y,'-o','linewidth', 4)

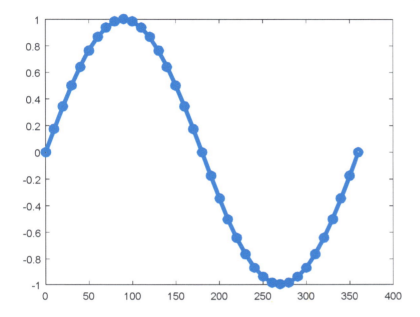

Here, the width of the line is 4. Other values can be used; the larger the value, the thicker the line, and vice versa.

The same is applicable to the size of the markers. We can change the size of the markers as follows:

plot(x,y,'-o','linewidth', 4, 'markersize', 9)

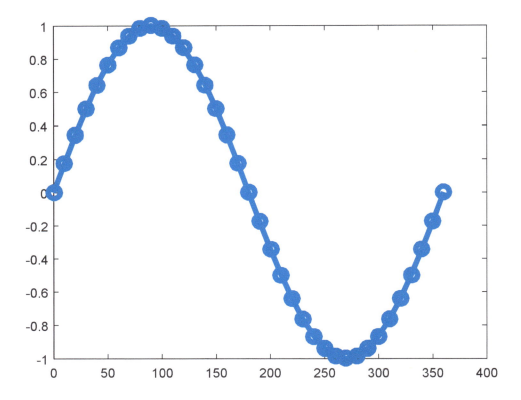

Here, the size of the marker is set to 9, and the plot is as illustrated below. This just changes the size of the circles (or whatever is used as the marker).

Note: We feel the illustration above is too thick (this is just for illustration purpose), you can adjust the values to sooth what you want to see.

Another interesting thing we can do is to change the color of the graph. By default, MATLAB uses blue for graphs, but we can change to other colors of our choice (e.g. red) by doing the following:

plot(x,y,'-or','linewidth', 4, 'markersize', 9)

Notice the newly included r, it changes the graph color to red as follows:

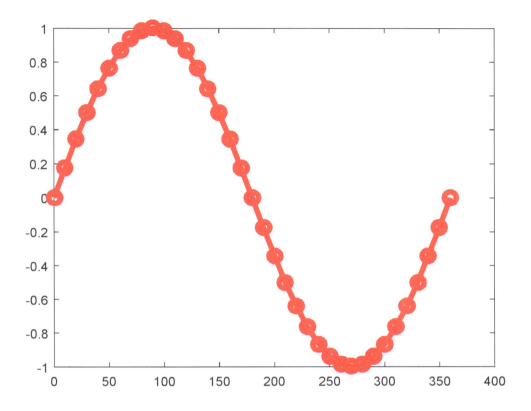

Other colors you may want to try include the following:

Color	How to specify on MATLAB
Blue	b
Yellow	y
Green	g
Magenta	m
Cyan	c
Black	k
White	w

If for instance, we do the following:

plot(x,y,'-og','linewidth', 4, 'markersize', 9)

We get a green plot as below because of the included g.

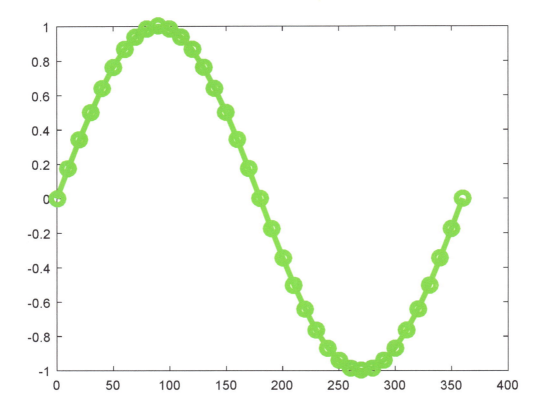

To add labels to the x and y axes, we add the following codes:

xlabel('Angle');
ylabel('Sine of Angle');

And the graph appears with x and y labels as below:

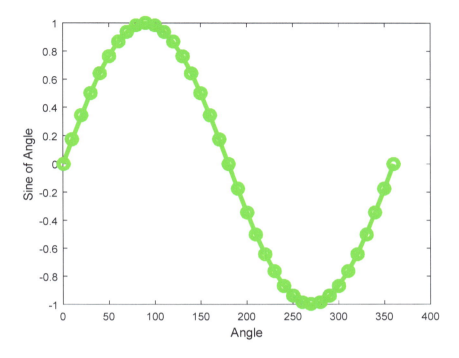

In a case where you need to add the title of the graph, you can do so as follows:

title('This Graph shows the Sine Curve')

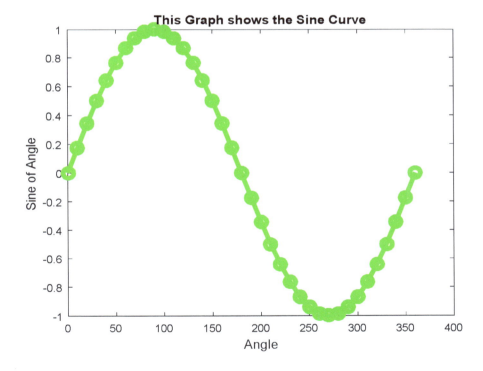

Finally on this section, we may want to decide the extent (or limits) of the x and y axes. In the figure above for example, the x limits go from 0 to 400, and the y limits go from -1 to 1. MATLAB does this automatically using the magnitude of values in the data to be plotted.

Interestingly, MATLAB allows us to redefine these limits supposing we don't like the default limits. To do this, let's suppose we prefer our x axis to go from 0 to 360, and our y axis to go from -1.2 to 1.2. Then we do the following:

xlim([0 360]);
ylim([-1.2 1.2]);

The graph now looks like below:

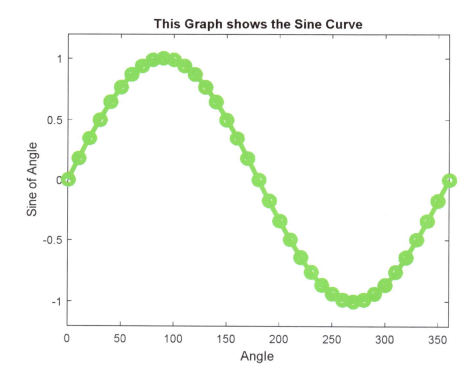

1.2 Making 2 or more Line Plots on the same Axis

Many at times, there is a need to plot 2 or more graphs on the same axis, especially when there is interest to visualize differences/similarities between two or more set of observations.

To do this, we just plot the first one, then ask MATLAB to hold on to the same figure. When we make subsequent plots, they'll all appear on the same axes. Let's illustrate by trying to make 3 plots (sine, cosine and tangent curves) on the same axes.

As usual, we first need to define our data. Let x still represent numbers from 0 to 360 in steps of 10. Then let ysine, ycosine, and ytangent respectively represent the sines, cosines, and tangents of the numbers in x. We define these in MATLAB as below:

```
x=0:10:360;
ysine=sind(x);
ycosine=cosd(x);
ytangent=tand(x);
```

Now to plot the sine curve in blue color with points plotted in asterisks, we use the command:

plot(x,ysine, '-*b');

The result is:

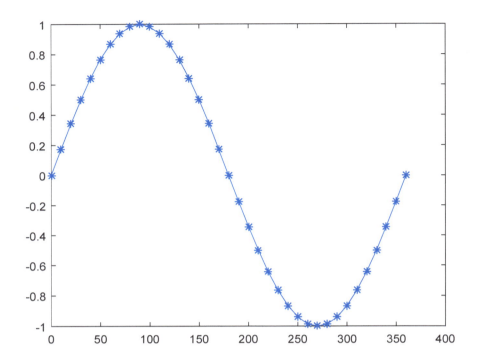

Then we ask MATLAB to hold on to this figure by using the following command (Note we do not need to close the figure created):

hold on;

Next, we want to add the cosine curve in red color and marked with circles. The command is as follows:

plot(x,ycosine, '-or');

And we get the following graph:

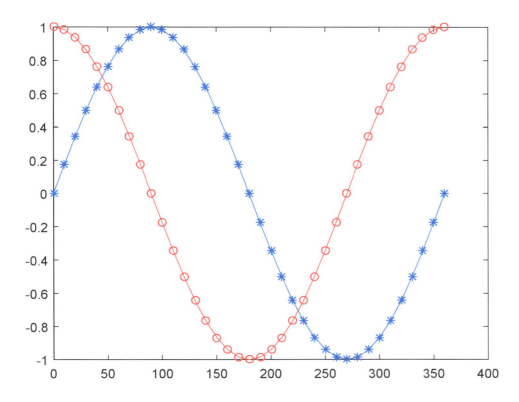

Finally, we add the tangent curve in green color and square markers using the following command:

plot(x,ytangent, '-sg');

And we get the final graph as below:

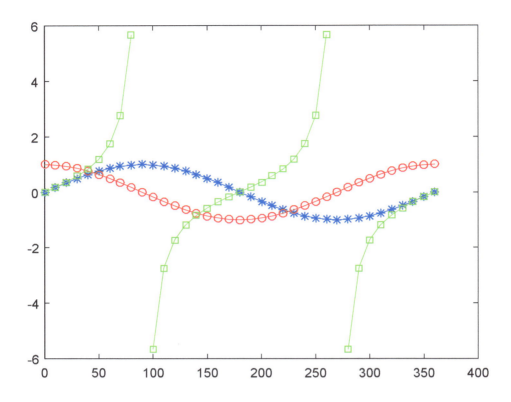

Something beautiful we will like to do is to add legends so as to make it easy for others to understand our illustrations. We do this using the following command:

legend('Sine Curve', 'Cosine Curve', 'Tangent Curve');

And we get the result as below:

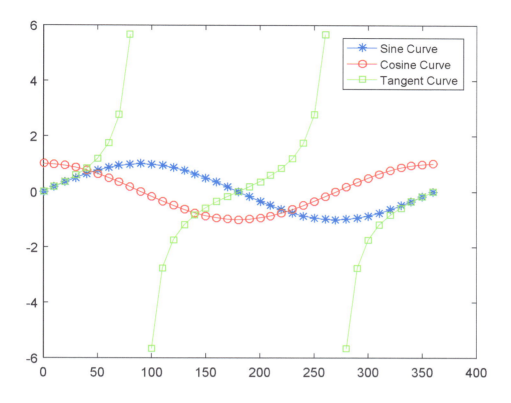

Observe the following about adding legends:

1. The strings in the bracket (that is, 'Sine Curve', 'Cosine Curve', 'Tangent Curve') can be any strings you want to appear on the legend, so feel free to try other strings.

2. The strings should be entered in the order the graphs were plotted. So for instance, if we plotted the tangent curve before the cosine curve, then the string for the tangent curve should appear before that of the cosine curve.

1.3 Making 2 Line Plots on the same x-Axis but different y-Axis

Sometimes we want to show two different quantities on the same plot. As an illustration, we want to see how temperature (in $^{\circ}$C) relates with solar radiation (in W/m^2) of a location over a day. It will not be great idea to plot both on the same y-axis since the magnitudes involved are far apart. Let's consider the measurements below.

Hour	Solar Radiation (W/m^2)	Temperature ($^{\circ}$C)
0	0.00	14.39
1	0.00	14.38
2	0.00	14.25
3	0.00	13.95
4	0.00	13.87
5	0.00	13.86
6	2.38	15.51
7	56.58	16.85
8	121.43	18.63
9	132.38	20.40
10	165.79	22.24
11	186.48	23.44
12	222.78	23.96
13	225.02	23.85
14	206.13	23.39
15	172.80	24.06
16	102.47	24.28
17	56.30	24.27
18	10.54	23.95
19	0.06	22.75
20	0.00	21.74
21	0.00	20.09
22	0.00	18.95
23	0.02	16.95

To plot the parameters on same x-axis but different y-axis, the MATLAB function required is 'plotyy'. We proceed this way:

First, copy and paste the data into the MATLAB environment, assigning it the name: data. To do this we type the following on either a MATLAB script or on the MATLAB command window:

data=[paste data here];

Next, we may choose to define data in the first, second, and third columns as hour, srad and temp respectively. This is done as shown below:

hour=data(:,1);
srad=data(:,2);
temp=data(:,3);

And finally, we create the plot using the 'plotyy' function as below:

plotyy(hour, srad, hour, temp);

The plot below is generated.

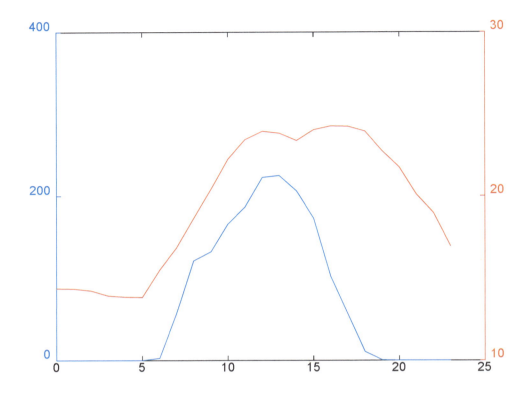

The syntax generally is:

plotyy(x1, y1, x2, y2);

where x1 and y1 are respectively for the left side of the plot, while x2 and y2 are for the right.

Additionally, we may want to modify various aspects of the plot, like axes labels, line schemes, etc. The ideas are very similar to what we have done earlier in this chapter.

1.4 Making Subplots

The idea here is to make different plots on same pane (something similar to grouping the plots).

For an illustration, we want to create something like this (a total of 6 plots in 3 rows and 2 columns):

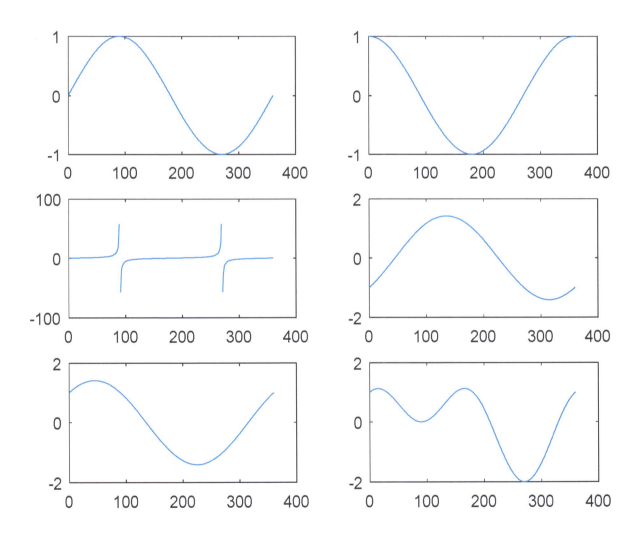

The MATLAB function required here is the 'subplot' function, and the syntax is as follows:

subplot(m.n,p), plot(xi,yi);

m is the number of rows of plots we want, while n is the number of columns. p is the postion of the plot we want to plot at the time. In the case above, for instance, where we have plots in 3 rows and 2 columns, m=3, n=2, and p changes from 1 to 6; p=1 when we want to make the 1st plot, 2 when we want to make the 2nd, etc.

Now, let's describe the production of the image above.

All the 6 plots have the same set of x-values, and that is; x going from 0 to 360. We define that in MATLAB as below:

x=0:360;

Then the y-values for each of the 6 plots are respectively defined as:

y1=sind(x);
y2=cosd(x);
y3=tand(x);
y4=sind(x)-cosd(x);
y5=sind(x)+cosd(x);
y6=sind(x)+cosd(2*x);

And finally, to create the plots, we use the commands below:

subplot(3,2,1), plot(x,y1);
subplot(3,2,2), plot(x,y2);
subplot(3,2,3), plot(x,y3);
subplot(3,2,4), plot(x,y4);
subplot(3,2,5), plot(x,y5);
subplot(3,2,6), plot(x,y6);